Remembering Rochester

Ruth Rosenberg Naparsteck

TURNER
PUBLISHING COMPANY

Sometime near the turn of the century, people look over the rail of the Court Street Bridge at the Genesee River, perhaps wondering if its waters will overrun the banks, which frequently happened in the spring. Flooding was considered an uncontrollable annual occurrence until the opening of the Mt. Morris Dam in the mid twentieth century.

Remembering
Rochester

Turner Publishing Company
4507 Charlotte Avenue • Suite 100
Nashville, Tennessee 37209
(615) 255-2665

Remembering Rochester

www.turnerpublishing.com

Library of Congress Control Number: 2010923494

ISBN: 978-1-59652-624-2

Printed in the United States of America

ISBN 978-1-68336-879-3 (pbk)

10 11 12 13 14 15 16—0 9 8 7 6 5 4 3 2

CONTENTS

Snow removal in Rochester and other lakeside communities in the north was a great challenge at the turn of the century. Heavy equipment was designed to plow and remove the snow to let emergency equipment pass through the streets. Fire fighters were especially challenged by the deep snows. Fortunately many of the heavy snowstorms occurred in the spring when snow melt was not far off.

Acknowledgments

This volume, *Remembering Rochester,* is the result of the cooperation and efforts of many individuals and organizations. It is with great thanks that we acknowledge in particular the valuable contribution of Rochester Public Library's City Hall Collection, Local History Collection, and Municipal Archives Collection.

———————

This project represents countless hours of review and research. The researchers and writer have reviewed thousands of photographs. We greatly appreciate the generous assistance of the archives listed here, without whom this project could not have been completed.

The goal in publishing this work is to provide broader access to a set of extraordinary photographs. The aim is to inspire, provide perspective, and evoke insight that might assist officials and citizens, who together are responsible for determining Rochester's future. In addition, the book seeks to preserve the past with respect and reverence.

With the exception of touching up imperfections that have accrued with the passage of time and cropping where necessary, no other changes have been made. The focus and clarity of many images is limited to the technology and the ability of the photographer at the time they were taken.

We encourage readers to reflect as they explore Rochester, stroll along its streets, or wander its neighborhoods. It is the publisher's hope that in making use of this work, longtime residents will learn something new and that new residents will gain a perspective on where Rochester has been, so that each can contribute to its future.

—*Todd Bottorff, Publisher*

INTRODUCTION

In *Sketches of Rochester,* the first real history of Rochester, Henry O'Reilly wrote in 1838 of the geological wealth and geographical advantages of the Genesee River Valley, upon which the city of Rochester is built at its outlet. The people, he wrote, need only take advantage of what was offered.

Coming from the New England states, the first white settlers brought with them the Puritan work ethic and the vision of a New England community that they set about reproducing both architecturally and culturally. There was work to be had by the wealthy entrepreneur as well as the barber who owned nothing more than a pair of scissors and a comb. The back-breaking labor of cutting wood, clearing trees for fields and roads, hauling stone, making bricks, and carting sawed lumber to building sites kept the unskilled settler busy.

Six settlements that eventually became Rochester, dotted the Genesee River's edge in the first decade of the nineteenth century. Each settlement believed it had the advantage that would make it the center of commerce. To name a few: Charlotte had the shipping port at its mouth, but ports nearer to the Lower Falls took away much of Charlotte's business; Carthage had a bridge that connected the east and west ends of Ridge Road, but the bridge collapsed after only fifteen months; Castletown lost its purpose as a transfer point when riverboats began to take the bypass to the Erie Canal; other settlements were not able to develop their assets before the rapid transformation of the One Hundred Acre Tract sealed their fate in the absorption of Frankfort into the formation of Rochesterville.

Colonel Nathaniel Rochester, the primary partner with William Fitzhugh and Charles Carrol, guided the One Hundred Acre Tract to become the path for the state road over the Main Street bridge and the Erie Canal aqueduct as well as the site of the Court House for newly formed Monroe County. The intersection of Main Street (toward Buffalo) and Lake Avenue (for shipping) ensured that both surface and lake travel would be centered in Rochesterville. Colonel Rochester helped to charter the village's own bank, which further stimulated growth. The opening of the Erie Canal in 1825 brought growth more rapid than anyone could have imagined. The fields to the south were so fertile that the grain sent to Rochester's mills made the Genesee River Valley the breadbasket of America. Lumber in the hills to the south helped to build boats and buildings.

Rochester was attractive to waves of immigrants who not only found Rochester a welcome home, but found a ready use for their skills. The assets the city held in the skills of its people alone made Rochester wealthy. This wide array of skills—in carpentry, masonry, brewing, shoe and clothing manufacture, agriculture and horticulture, optics and precision instruments—as well as the diversity of manufacturing they made possible, protected the city from the effects of economic downturns better than cities that depended on one industry.

The following collection of photographs reveals the city over a century as it grew from adolescence in the mid nineteenth century to maturity shortly after the mid twentieth century. In 2006, still on the leading edge of technology, innovation, medical science, and education, Rochester is seeking a redefinition of its image. This collection is published with a view toward that goal.

Built in 1852 to replace the wooden Auburn Railroad Station, this New York Central Railroad Station stood until 1883 when it was replaced with a more modern edifice. Abraham Lincoln stopped near this station in 1860 on his way to Washington to take the oath of office as president of the United States. Five years later his funeral train came through. First Lady Mary Lincoln also passed through Rochester, dining at the Waverly House seen on the right.

FROM CIVIL WAR TO GROWING CITY

(1865–1879)

This early 1860s locomotive was named for David Upton (1816–1885), once master mechanic and superintendent in the western division for New York Central Railroad. In 1865, Upton arranged for several railroad cars to carry dignitaries joining the funeral cortege of the assassinated president Abraham Lincoln.

The floodwaters of the Genesee River in 1865 were carried north through the Genesee Valley Canal and east and west through the Erie Canal. The gas company feared gas explosions in the public street lamps, but fortunately no fires or explosions erupted. This photograph emphasizes the depth of the waters.

Following the Civil War, a Victory Arch was erected over Main Street near the Four Corners at State Street. Local nurseryman Edward Allen Frost financed the arch, which cheered "Long Live the Republic" while individually recognizing the contributions of six men who served.

The *American Rural Home* and the German language *Rochester Beobachter* newspapers were published in the Rochester Evening Express Building at the southwest corner of Aqueduct and west Main (then Buffalo) streets in the early 1870s. Evening Express building owners C. D. Tracy and F. S. Rew leased to other businesses, like the Cigar and Tobacco Manufactory of Solomon F. Hess and the busy hardware store of Arthur S. Hamilton and James W. McKindley.

Ice skaters enjoy late-afternoon recreation among canal boats tied up for the winter on the Erie Canal aqueduct in the early 1800s. In season between May and late November, this aqueduct bed was busy with boat traffic.

The busy intersection of Main and State streets, known as the Four Corners, was the site of a stone building in 1818. Expanded several times, the five-story building was known as the Burns Block about 1846. In 1864, the name changed to the Elwood Block. It was demolished and replaced with the Elwood Building in 1879. Photographed here before 1879, the Elwood Block is leased to tailor Timothy Derrick, dentist John F. Sanford, and jeweler Elias S. Ettenheimer.

People said Abelard Reynolds took a great financial risk building the Reynolds Arcade in 1828. The four-story building cost $30,000, making it the largest, most expensive building west of the Hudson River. Just a decade after Rochester became a village, the arcade became the center of activity, housing a post office, Western Union, and Dewey's Books. Pictured here about 1877, this building stood until 1932, when it was demolished and replaced with the second Reynolds Arcade.

A City of Immigrants

(1880–1899)

This view north from the Four Corners at State Street and Main about 1880 shows the nearly locking traffic of the busy downtown as wagons, horse-drawn streetcars, and pedestrians make their way through. A policeman stands in the street to help maintain order. The Powers Building can be seen on the left and the new Elwood Building on the right. State Street, which becomes Lake Avenue, was one of the first plank roads constructed.

Residents in the city commonly had their milk delivered daily by local farmers, who rose in the wee hours of the morning to provide that service. Many houses in the city still have milk delivery doors near the side or rear doors. This photograph (from 1880 or before) shows Josh Kintz on the left and Milton Kintz seated on the sleigh.

Near the intersection of Monroe Avenue and the Erie Canal, the C. C. Meyer and Son Steam Sawmill filled orders for lumber and building supplies for buildings and boats in the growing city of Rochester. One buckboard wagon is loaded with lumber as its passengers wait. A young girl in a dress in the foreground is possibly waiting for an order to be filled.

The Elwood Building can be seen at left in this view of Main Street looking east from the Four Corners. The Reynolds Arcade is still a center to the city's busy commerce and communications seen here in the 1880s. The horse-drawn streetcars have given way to electric streetcars and telephone lines now crisscross the city's streets.

In the early 1900s, Driving Park Race Track attracted hundreds to watch the sulky races. Two sulky drivers race past the judges' stand in this photograph from around the turn of the century. When the horse races ended, dog races were held for a few seasons before they were banned. Once a part of Greece, New York, the land occupied by Driving Park became a part of the city.

As residents of the city moved farther from downtown, horse-drawn streetcars filled the need for mass transportation. This Rochester City and Brighton Railroad Company began in 1863. In 1890, it sold to the Rochester Railway Company, which electrified the line. Fewer people kept their own horses and buggies as the city grew, relying instead on the streetcars and liveries.

A rare view of Aqueduct Street from the south side of East Main Street shows loaded wagons and busy pedestrians in front of businesses like C. F. Weaver and Sons, Louis Ernst and Son, and J. C. Barnard.

A policeman stands watch at the intersection of Main and Fitzhugh streets across from the Powers Building between 1883 and 1885. The famous Coggswell Fountain, placed at the front of the Monroe County Court House by temperance-minded Henry Coggswell, is visible at right. By this time, Rochester had been a city for half a century and was home to newly arriving German and Italian immigrants.

Hundreds of people gathered outside the second Monroe County Court House for the funeral of Lieutenant Frederick F. Kislingbury, who died on the arctic expedition of Adolphus Greely in 1884. Second in command, Kislingbury died of starvation along with several others in his unit, after a supply boat was unable to reach their ice-locked location. A few of his men survived to be rescued and rumors of cannibalism circulated. Kislingbury's remains were exhumed from his grave at Mt. Hope Cemetery. An autopsy confirmed cannibalism in one of America's most tragic expeditions.

Several people stand in the doorway of wholesale milliner Joseph Shatz on State Street. A little off balance and without a hat, a woman's dress is displayed in front of the business next door. Women's hats were fashionable in the late nineteenth century. Many immigrant and single or widowed women in Rochester learned to make hats in night school.

Bartholomay Cottage Hotel, run by Bartholomay Brewery, was a popular nineteenth-century site for picnics and other celebrations on Lake Ontario. One happy party poses for a photograph on a six-horse-drawn "carryall" wagon in front of the hotel.

S. R. Newborn Feed Store displays a stenciled advertisement facing the Genesee River. Shown here are the backsides of deteriorating buildings along South St. Paul Street between Court Street and the Erie Canal aqueduct. (ca. 1875–1893)

Several horse-drawn wagons wait for the signal to cross the West Avenue lift bridge at the Erie Canal. This bridge replaced the old swing bridge. The sign warns carriage drivers of a $25 fine for driving on the bridge after the gong sounds, alerting them that the bridge will be lifted.

This second Monroe County Court House was built in 1850 and demolished in 1894 to make way for the third Court House, now referred to as the Monroe County Office Building. Old City Hall is in the background at right.

Main Street facing west about 1888. Worden's Eating House, Garson's Department Store, the Elwood Building, and the Powers Building are visible on the north side of the street. The Wilder Building is on the south side at left.

On February 18, 1887, a severe storm with heavy winds tore out a section of the Court Street bridge, pulling out the paving planks and wire poles. Curious spectators stand precariously at the edge of a fallen section, heedless of the story of a woman swept over the bridge and drowned when the bridge was damaged.

The beautiful Rochester Free Academy stands across from the peaceful plaza between old City Hall and the second Monroe County Court House. St. Luke's Church is visible on the left next to the academy. The plaza is gone, but all of these buildings still stand today.

The Monroe Commandery No. 12 of the Knights of Templar, dressed in full uniform, practice precision drills at an unnamed location around the turn of the century.

In this view west down Main Street, wagons and a streetcar are seen in the background at the intersection of East Avenue. In the foreground, street construction appears to be under way. (ca. 1890)

Rochester Railway Company's Car No. 112 was the first electric streetcar to run in the city of Rochester. The red and yellow car ran along Lake Avenue on its first run in November 1890. In 1909, the company merged with New York State Railways.

Driver Edward Klippert and engineer Frank J. Brennan, at rear, display Rochester Fire Department's Steamer No. 2 on North Clinton Avenue near Lowell Street. At left is the corner of Hose Company No. 2 and Steamer No. 2.

A young girl sits astride a pony in this view of the German Theological Seminary at Alexander and Tracy streets (ca. 1890). This is probably the newer of two buildings on this site.

The Rochester School for the Deaf about 1890 at 263 North St. Paul Street. Established in 1874 by Mrs. Gilman Perkins, the school offered innovative education to the hearing impaired. Instruction in speech and sign language was innovative and became known as the Rochester method. Alexander Graham Bell visited Rochester and worked with the school on several occasions. The school is still located on St. Paul Street.

Clinton Avenue was once lined with movie theaters. About 1890 a man stands in the entrance of the Lyceum Theatre, built in 1888 by Rochester architects Warner and Brockett on a design by Leon Lempert. It was one of the largest in the nation. The posters on the sidewalk beckon passers-by into the theater. The building was razed in 1934.

Established in 1842 as Woodbury, Morse and Company, this art-supply store at the corner of East Main and Graves streets became Smith and Hollister in 1889. In this photograph taken about 1893, varnish barrels are stacked in front of the store. Window sashes, doors, and blinds are available in the business upstairs.

A young boy runs westward along Main Street at North Water Street in April of 1893. An electric streetcar passes by on tracks raised above the brick street surface. The gutter at the side of the street helps to drain the rainwater, which formerly sat stagnant with horse droppings. A stone step from the sidewalk to the street helps pedestrians avoid the mud on rainy days.

A larger-than-life statue of Abraham Lincoln stands atop the Soldiers and Sailors Monument at the dedication May 30, 1892, at Washington Square near the intersection of Court Street and Clinton and South avenues. The monument was designed by Leonard Volk. Hundreds of people dressed patriotically for the occasion.

Driver John Hammond required a lot of skill to manage this six-horse team and their new fire truck seen here in 1895 in the doorway of the Hook and Ladder Company No. 1 on Front Street. Standing at right is probably Captain Patrick O'Meara.

At the turn of the century two young boys drive a pony cart to School no. 26.

Penny farthing bicyclists pass spectators in a 4th of July parade on East Main Street in downtown Rochester. New York Cloak and Fur Company and Salter Brothers Florist are visible in the background.

Signs for Oliver's and Ward's chilled plows and farming implements advertise the agricultural tools that could be purchased or repaired in this Penfield building that was John A. Schueler's blacksmith shop in the 1890s.

The Powers Hotel and Powers Building on the left dominate Main Street in this view facing east from Fitzhugh Street near the Monroe County Court House.

Looking south from the Driving Park Bridge, the graceful bend of the Lower Falls is seen dropping the Genesee River about 80 feet to a more leisurely flow. The first Carthage Bridge was built on this site in 1818 to connect the east and west portions of the Ridge Road. It fell after 15 months, crashing the financial hopes of its investors.

The Whitcomb House, the Temperance Hotel, the Granite Building, and the Powers buildings are visible in this view of Main Street looking west from Clinton Avenue. The street is busy with wagons, a bicycle, pedestrians, and a streetcar.

At the intersection of Main and State streets looking northeast, horses stand blanketed as men work to remove snow from the Four Corners near the Elwood Building. (1890s)

This seven-story Elwood Building, built by Frank Elwood in memory of Isaac R. Elwood in 1879, cost $100,000, at the time a vast sum. The shop of opticians E. E. Bausch and Sons occupied the ground floor. The Powers Building is across State Street at left. Numerous bicycles, here and in other images, suggest that this mode of travel was relied on by many.

Looking west on Monroe Avenue from Manhattan Street, in front of Charles M. Roalman's Market and Edward Rabe's Harness Shop, a surveyor stands among workmen who lay paving bricks on the roadbed and fit them snugly along the streetcar tracks.

Looking east along the Erie Canal from Plymouth Avenue in winter. Wind-blown snowdrifts pile against the buildings. The pointed bell tower of old City Hall at center and the square steeple of St. Luke's Church at left are visible. The Fitzhugh Street Bridge across the canal was built in 1899 by the Rochester Bridge and Iron Works.

Looking south toward Hotel Ontario and the Auditorium Theatre, the beach can be seen at left. The park is busy with visitors, present to enjoy concerts, exhibitions, rides, fireworks, and refreshments. (1890s)

The Erie Canal flows quiet in this 1880s photograph looking north toward Court Street.

The school founded by J. Howard Bradstreet and Elden G. Burritt in 1891 operated until 1907. Posing for the camera is a Bradstreet hockey team.

Identified only as Tessie, Amelia, and Fred, these three people enjoy the day on the Charlotte boardwalk at Charlotte Beach on Lake Ontario on July 28, 1899. Until nearly the middle of the twentieth century, people went to the beach in full dress or full-body bathing suits, even in the heat of July. The cooler breezes off the lake gave respite to people from the city. A "fresh air" program brought poor children from the city to the lake in the summer to keep them healthy.

Looking east from the Chamber of Commerce Building, nearly the entire length of Main Street east can be seen in this photograph taken about 1900.

GREAT EXPECTATIONS
(1900–1919)

The popularity of bicycles is apparent in this view of East Main Street looking west toward St. Paul Street (1900). The Granite Building is at right and the Burke Building is at center. Electric streetcars reduced the number of wagons crowding city streets. One newspaper complained that the cost of bicycles would keep people from buying them and no one would buy from a businessman who made a sales call on a bicycle.

Though the bicycle was predicted to be unsuccessful, by the 1890s there were more than 40,000 in use in Monroe County, and bicycle clubs formed spawning the construction of bicycle paths through Rochester area parks. The bicycle was welcomed by women who enjoyed a newfound freedom of movement.

A man dressed in a business suit crosses West Main Street. In this view looking east the length of Main Street, the Powers Building can be seen in the distance.

One horse-drawn carriage bears a sign "The Livingston," probably taking the hotel Livingston's guests to and from this New York Central Railroad Station on Central Avenue. Other carriages await in the lot along Central Avenue looking west from North Clinton Avenue. Several hotels, a barber shop, billiards rooms, and other businesses line Central Avenue to serve train passengers.

Civil War veterans of the Grand Army of the Republic, probably Reynolds Battery, pose with their horse-drawn cannon around 1900.

The words "Not the Last Stroke but Every Stroke Brings Victory" are written on the Triumphal Arch built to honor General Elwell Otis on his return from the Spanish-American War about 1900. The arch stood at the corner of East Avenue and Main Street.

The Empire Theatre stands on the northeast corner of East Main Street and North Clinton Avenue on what became the site of the new Sibley's Store after 1904. Signs on the front upper level advertise burlesque, farce comedy, vaudeville, and melodrama. Cooper's Drug Store occupies the street level.

The Granite Building can be seen at center in the distance. Several bicyclists travel along Main Street. Wagons line the north side of the street.

At Main Street near
South Clinton Avenue,
an early-twentieth-
century parade breaks
up at the end of the
parade route. Flag
bunting hangs in
celebration from the
buildings. Streetcars
wait to resume their
routine schedule.

The intersection of Lake Avenue near Ridge Road became known as Wagg's Corners, a landmark to area residents, after Gilbert J. Wagg opened his department store on the east side in 1905. In 1912, he moved the store to the southwest corner. In a fairly new retail concept, the department store offered meats, groceries, dry goods, shoes, hardware, and furniture under one roof. The business operated until 1964 and the building was demolished in 1988.

Pedestrians walk along the sidewalk on what appears to be a rainy day in 1909 on South Clinton Avenue between Main and Court streets. Several automobiles are parked across the street.

Main Street facing east from the Four Corners in 1910. The Powers Building can be seen on the left and the Rochester Trust and Safe Deposit Company on the right. The rain creates a gloomy mood in the city as the streetcars pass by. Horse-drawn wagons wait at the curb for their drivers.

People look out the windows and from the balcony of the Powers Building as hundreds line the streets to watch the Labor Day parade in 1910. Flags fly from the buildings. Labor unions were strong and active in the Rochester area early in the century.

Mr. and Mrs. Moses Sharp stand in front of their commission house on Front Street about 1910. Farmers and hunters brought game and farm animals to Sharp's Commission House for processing and sale on commission. On Saturdays Sharp sold meat at retail.

John Frisbie prepares a second test flight the year of his death. Frisbie was one of several aviation pioneers in the Rochester area. (1911)

Wearing a top hat, president William Howard Taft looks down from the review stand on the Grand Army of the Republic parade on the south side of the Soldiers and Sailors Monument at Washington Square Park. Hundreds crowded the park and viewed the parade in August 1911.

Looking south from the Steamboat Pier at the Pier Hotel (left) in Sea Breeze.

The Church of the Blessed Sacrament, designed by Gordon and Madden, was dedicated in 1912 on Oxford Street near Monroe Avenue. The church replaced an earlier church on the same site.

Laborers work to lay streetcar tracks along Dewey Avenue from Ravine Avenue. In the distance a streetcar crosses near Glendale Park. (August 1913)

Probably during the flood of March 28, 1913, this photograph shows the backside of Front Street businesses enduring the dangerous river waters threatening the foundations of buildings. Myer's Department Store, Charles Adam (a grinder), Zweigle's (a sausage maker and saloon), and the Weis and Fisher Company are visible from 27 to 52 Front Street.

The 300-room fireproof Hotel Rochester was built by Walter B. Duffy on the southeast corner of West Main Street and Plymouth Avenue in 1908. Designed by architects Charles F. Crandall and John F. Strobel, the eight-story building was a hotel until 1957, when it became dormitories for students at Rochester Institute of Technology. The ten-foot-wide main entrance on West Main Street was bordered by an ornamental cast-iron marquee. The women's entrance was on Plymouth Avenue. The hotel offered a ladies reception room and parlor, billiards room, and a men's cafe.

The stone wall of the Erie Canal below South Avenue. When the canal was emptied at the end of the season in 1919, subway tracks were run through its bed. In 1936, the Rundel Memorial Building housing the Rochester Public Library was built over it, supported by steel beams and accessible from South Avenue. The Osburn Hotel, on the site of today's library addition, is more visible in this view. (ca. 1914)

Street-paving bricks lie in piles for laborers working on Curtice Street near St. Paul Street. A city engineer car parked at the intersection may indicate a job inspection or supervision. The Bartholomay Brewing Company building is on the right. (June 1914)

Principal Maude West led students from the Irondequoit Union Free School in support of Prohibition in November 1915. They participated in a flag-waving Prohibition parade. Here they are seen in a truck crossing Titus Avenue in Irondequoit. Maude West is seated next to the driver. She became Irondequoit's first town historian in 1922 when the New York State Education Law first required every town and village to appoint a historian.

Most likely sewers and retaining walls built in response to earlier floods prevented the flood of March-April 1916 from becoming more damaging. Spring snowmelts brought unusually high water levels to the city as seen here on Exchange Street downtown. Though a current can be seen in the floodwaters, business continues.

Organized in 1903, the Rochester Chapter of the American Red Cross established a canteen at the New York Central Railroad Station during World War I to offer refreshments and friendship to soldiers passing through Rochester. This group photograph of Red Cross canteen workers was taken sometime during World War I.

This view faces northeast from the southwest corner of Main and Clinton streets toward the Sibley Department Store. The local landmark Sibley clock tower is visible above the store in this 1916 photograph.

Just north of the Bausch Bridge on the east side of the Genesee River, this Bausch and Lomb Glass Plant produced eye-glass products. During World War I the plant produced optical glass for the military.

The Rochester Parks Department worked with the library to bring books to children to check out to encourage reading. In 1917, children line up in the playground of School No. 36 as the librarian checks out the books. Story hours also were held in the city's playgrounds.

Students in the U.S. School of Aerial Photography at Kodak Park learned photography and camera repair from March to December 1918. More than 2,000 servicemen were taught aerial reconnaissance, but World War I ended before they were assigned to combat units.

At a rally to sell war bonds during World War I, Bertha Eldridge challenges the crowd to do their patriotic duty and buy the bonds. She and other women worked as Minute Women until the war ended.

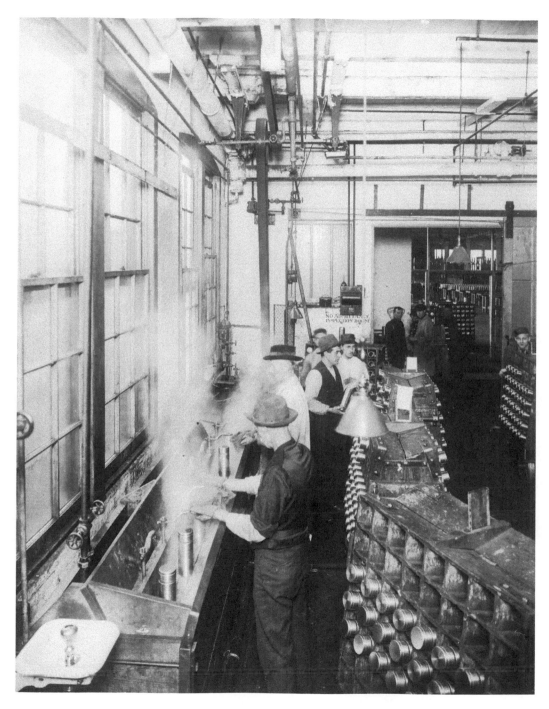

Employees at T. H. Symington Company work to manufacture up to 15,000 shell casings and sockets a day; first for the British during World War I, then for the United States when it entered the war.

Celebrating Armistice Day, a group of patriotic people crowd a flag-draped truck to travel through the city's streets celebrating the end of World War I. The sign in the front reads, "We got the Kaiser in the Cage."

About 6,000 mothers of military personnel in World War I were honored at Exposition Park with a medal. If a mother lost a son, her medal bore the gold star that represented their loss. Gold Star mothers displayed a gold star in the windows of their homes. Sadly, some mothers displayed more than one star.

Often referred to as the Burke Building, Burke, Fitzsimons, Hone and Company opened in 1849 and remained in business until 1919. Burke stands next door to McFarlin's Clothing Company at 110-116 Main Street. Francis M. McFarlin opened his clothing store in 1860 and remained in business at various locations until 1983.

A rider successfully completes a difficult jump as his horse clears a 7-foot-4-inch rail. Men hold the rail in place as judges look on in the horse-jumping competition at the Rochester Exposition. (September 3, 1919)

The Rochester Exposition of 1919 attracted hundreds of people to exhibition tents, food stands, and a variety of entertainment. The Ferris wheel in the background was certainly one of the most popular attractions. (September 3, 1919)

Construction laborers work on the New York State Barge Canal in the early 1900s. The Erie Canal was moved from downtown Rochester in 1918–1919 to the Genesee Valley Park, where it crossed the Genesee River at grade level rather than over an aqueduct as it had downtown. The section of the Genesee River from the canal crossing to the Court Street Dam became a part of the canal system.

Before World War II mass transportation was important in local travel. On the northeast corner of Court and Exchange streets, the Rochester and Eastern Rapid Railway and the Rochester and Sodus Bay Railway operated out of this Electric Passenger and Express Service building until 1927. The building was demolished in 1951 to make way for the Rochester War Memorial.

Rochester Rises to the Challenge

(1920–1939)

Architect Daniel Loomis designed this house on the southeast corner of Spring and South Washington streets for Thomas Hart Rochester, son of the city's founder, Colonel Nathaniel Rochester. Thomas was the sixth mayor of Rochester. Mary Bliss later ran a school in the house before it became a dormitory and fraternity house for Mechanics Institute, predecessor of today's Rochester Institute of Technology. In 1921, about the time this photograph was taken, the Locust Club purchased the house.

The statue of the University of Rochester's first president, Martin Brewer Anderson, stands on the Prince Street campus. The statue was created by J. Guernsey Mitchell, who also created the statue of Mercury that stands today on the Rochester skyline. The statue of Anderson was later moved to the university's River Street campus. This Prince Street site became the women's campus. To the left is the Sibley Building. On the right is Anderson Hall.

Across Broad Street from Fitzhugh Street, old City Hall was used from 1875 to 1978, when city officials moved to the old Federal Building at Church and Fitzhugh streets. In the foreground is George Higgins's business, where automobiles were rebuilt or repaired. Higgins set up his business as a carriage repair shop, but as many other mechanics like him discovered, it was necessary to change with the times in order to stay in business.

Architect Claude Bragdon designed the First Universalist Church at Court Street and Clinton Avenue near Washington Square Park in 1908. It replaced the church that was razed to make way for the nearby Seneca Hotel.

In the early 1920s laborers work on the subway at the east end of the Broad Street Bridge. The subway ran through the old Erie Canal bed after the canal was relocated to the Genesee Valley Park on the south border of the city. A road deck was built over the old canal bed so that automobiles could travel above the new subway. In 1956, the subway was abandoned, and today numerous plans propose various uses for it.

Six firemen were injured
fighting the fire at the
Lawless Paper Company
on North Water Street in
April 1924.

Crowds wait to enter as Exposition Park General Manager Edgar Edwards and Mayor Clarence Van Zandt open the gate to officially kick off the 1925 Rochester Exposition.

In this view looking southwest across Allen and Fitzhugh streets, the Brick Presbyterian Church is visible as it appeared around 1924. The north tower, with its ten-foot illuminated Roman Cross, replaced the Gothic steeples on top of the church destroyed by fire in 1903.

Abraham H. and Joseph M. Neisner started this discount variety store in 1911 in Rochester and franchised it four decades later in more than 100 locations in the United States. Neisner's merged with Ames in 1978 and was bought out by McCrory's in 1980.

This view faces southeast from the corner of South Clinton and Monroe avenues in the early 1920s.

The Eastman School of Music, part of the University of Rochester, opened with the Eastman Theatre in 1921 on Gibbs Street at Main. The Eastman School often broadcast from WHAM Radio, whose tower is visible in the background.

The first airmail was picked up in Rochester on June 1, 1928, after a test run. Early Rochester aviators demonstrated the usefulness of airplanes in the first two decades of the twentieth century. Regular passenger service was not far behind.

Cars had been passing over the Broad Street Bridge for less than a decade when this aerial photograph was taken over the Genesee River (ca. 1929). North of the Court Street Bridge (at bottom) are the Broad Street Bridge, the built-over Main Street Bridge, the New York Central Railroad Bridge, the Platt Street Bridge (today Pont de Rennes pedestrian bridge), and the RG&E footbridge near their old power-generating plant.

After its last season downtown in 1918, the Erie Canal was rerouted to cross the Genesee River at grade level south of the city in Genesee Valley Park. The old aqueduct was revamped for vehicular traffic and a subway was run along the old canal bed underneath the street. In the image, the Osburn Hotel stands where today Broad Street is extended. To the left is the Blue Bus Lines Terminal.

Founded in 1854, the University of Rochester began in downtown Rochester and later built a beautiful campus centered on Prince Street. The university moved in 1930 to the River Campus. The building with the dome in the center background is Rush Rhees Library, named for the man who served as president from 1900 to 1935. He persuaded Kodak founder George Eastman to donate millions of dollars to the university.

This aerial view of the city around Kodak Park shows the intersection of Lake Avenue on the right and Ridge Road on the left. At the time, Kodak was the chief employer in the Rochester area. Few people had not worked for Kodak or were not related to someone who did.

The first Reynolds Arcade was built by Abelard Reynolds in 1828. It was at the time the largest commercial building west of the Hudson River. It housed the first post office, Western Union Telegraph, Dewey Book Store, and the infant Bausch and Lomb Company. Many abolitionists and temperance advocates raised money there among the many businesses. This building was demolished in 1932 to make way for the Art Deco building by the same name that now stands on the site.

About 1935 a man and woman stand in front of No. 7 Clinton Avenue, where there was a beauty shop, a dance studio, and Hall-Covell men's furnishings. Clinton Avenue was also known at the time for its wonderful cinema theaters.

Known popularly as the Rochester Free Academy, this building on South Fitzhugh Street was first used as Rochester's first public high school in 1874. From 1905 to 1926, it housed city offices as the Municipal Building. The Rochester City School District began to use it after 1926. It stands next to the pioneer St. Luke and St. Simon Cyrene Episcopal Church (once St. Luke's Episcopal Church).

In the mid-1930s, men struggle to remove snow from downtown streets. Snowstorms were dreaded before the advent of powerful equipment to clear emergency paths for fire and ambulance vehicles. Excess snow was dumped over the bridges into the Genesee River. Some days the city was nearly brought to a stand-still. People today who complain about the inconvenience and damage wrought by snowstorms may have little idea what residents went through a century ago.

Secret Servicemen and patrolmen on motorcycles or horses flank the motorcade of President Franklin Delano Roosevelt and First Lady Eleanor Roosevelt in an October 1936 visit to Rochester. Despite a light rain, crowds turned out to greet the president, who was at the helm through the Great Depression.

Pedestrians cross the Genesee River over the Court Street Bridge as water rushes against the supports. The Rochester Public Library in the Rundel Memorial Building stands (in the background) on metal supports above what was once the subway system, anchoring the south end of downtown.

On October 4, 1936, the long awaited Rochester Public Library was dedicated in the Rundel Memorial Building at South Avenue between Broad and Court streets. The library system was unusual in that it had branch libraries long before it had this central library. Many people who had either lost their employment or needed to retrain for other jobs, trained themselves through the library's facilities.

The Sibley, Lindsay and Curr Department Store at night around Christmas 1939, showing Christmas a century earlier in the window displays. The store was a success from its beginning in 1868. The store expanded downtown and in 1893 moved into the Granite Building, where it remained until the great Sibley fire of 1904 gutted the building. The business then moved to a new location on Main Street between Clinton and North streets, pulling the hub of downtown farther east.

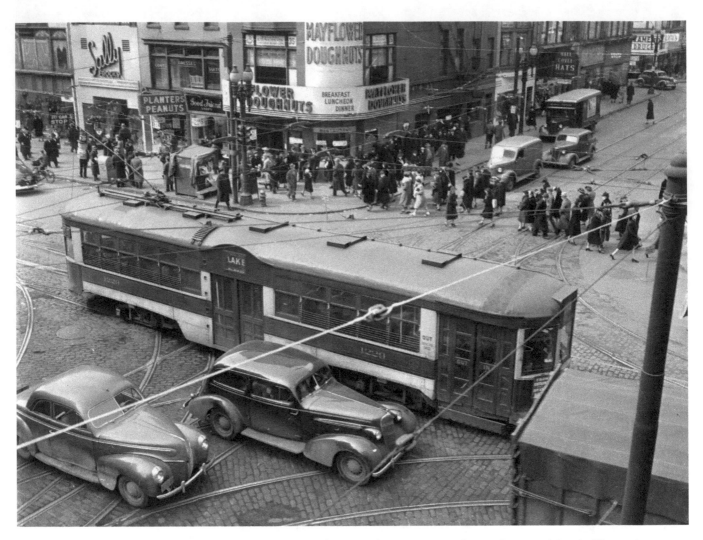

On the brink of World War II, the streets of downtown Rochester at the intersection of Main Street and South Clinton Avenue are busy with shoppers, cars, delivery trucks, and streetcars. Tracks crisscrossing around the cobbled roads point up continuing reliance on the streetcar.

United to Win the War
(1940–1949)

Several people look at the photographer as they board the streetcar on East Main Street around 1941. The driver must watch carefully for anyone in the roadway. The sign near the door says, "Front entrance—Pay as you enter." Neisner Brothers Dime Store and Stephen's Women's Clothing are visible at right.

Mrs. Robert McGlashan places her donated books into the tent set up for the "Victory Book Campaign." Similar drop-off points were set up at libraries throughout the area. Between January 12 and 24, 1942, the joint effort of the American Library Association, American Red Cross, and the United Service Organization sought to collect ten million books. Three million were reportedly gathered. People continued to donate after the campaign ended.

A motorcycle policeman strides past a streetcar on East Main Street near Clinton Avenue. The Monroe Savings Bank is visible across the street. Streetcar drivers had to be very alert to pedestrians such as the man crossing the street in the foreground. Passengers boarded in the street and could be struck by the streetcar or other vehicles as they crossed to the sidewalk.

Looking east down Main Street from the Four Corners intersection of Main and State streets. The corner of the Powers Building is visible at left and the Wilder Building is diagonally across the street. The Elwood Building, across Main Street from the Wilder Building, is left of center. (September 13, 1946)

Shoppers gaze in the store windows and make purchases along East Main Street in the years after World War II. Along the street from the left are Baker's Shoes, the Darling Shop (women's clothing), Neisner Brothers Five Cents to a Dollar, and a glimpse of Stephen's Women's Clothing Store.

Two women prepare to board the city subway at Exchange and Broad streets as passengers prepare to step off at the City Hall station on October 22, 1945.

East Main Street near St. Paul Street is busy with shoppers on October 6, 1947. F. W. Woolworth stands on the corner of Clinton and Main in the Granite Building that once housed the old Sibley, Lindsay and Curr Store before it burned in 1904. At right is the H. L. Green Five and Dime Store. Edwards and Son Department Store is next door.

On the centennial of Susan B. Anthony's arrival in Rochester, a memorial marker was erected at her house at 17 Madison Street. Shown from left to right are Mayor Samuel Dicker, Susan B. Anthony III, Martha Howard, and Caroline Gannett. Anthony shared the home with her sister, Mary, until their deaths in 1906 and 1909, respectively. The Rochester Federation of Women's Clubs purchased the home for the Susan B. Anthony Memorial and it is today a museum.

On South Avenue from East Main Street are, at left, Rudolph's Jewelers and Opticians and the South Avenue entrance to Bond Clothing. At right is the Main Street entrance to Walgreen Drugs. The Embassy Theatre and Georgia's Restaurant are farther down South Avenue.

The Rochester Museum of Arts and Sciences (today Rochester Museum and Science Center) chartered buses to send as many as 60 children between the ages of 6 and 16 on nature hikes over a six-week period in the summer of 1949. City schools worked with the Parent and Teacher Association to sponsor the children for the day trips. Here, Marion Peake, head of the school service at the museum, helps children board the bus on July 6.

On March 24, 1948, a passenger plane sits outside the terminal at the Rochester Municipal Airport on Scottsville Road. Since before the Wright brothers made the first flight at Kitty Hawk, North Carolina, Rochester had aviation pioneers. With the advent of powered flight, pastures became airfields and soon commercial airports were constructed. Today several airline companies fly jets from the Rochester International Airport.

NOTES ON THE PHOTOGRAPHS

These notes, listed by page number, attempt to include all aspects known of the photographs. Each of the photographs is identified by the page number, a title or description, photographer and collection, archive, and call or box number when applicable. Although every attempt was made to collect all data, in some cases complete data may have been unavailable due to the age and condition of some of the photographs and records.

II COURT STREET BRIDGE
Rochester Public Library
Local History Division
rpf00635

VI SNOW ON STATE STREET
Rochester Public Library
Local History Division
rpf00096

X NEW YORK CENTRAL RAILROAD STATION
Rochester Public Library
Local History Division
rpf01887

2 DAVID UPTON LOCOMOTIVE
Rochester Public Library
Local History Division
rpf00684

3 FLOODWATERS, 1865
Rochester Public Library
Local History Division
rpf01744

4 CIVIL WAR ARCH
Rochester Public Library
Local History Division
rpf00500

5 ROCHESTER EVENING EXPRESS
Rochester Public Library
Local History Division
rpf01556

6 ICE SKATERS ON ERIE CANAL
Rochester Public Library
Local History Division
rpf01103

7 OLD ELWOOD BLOCK
Rochester Public Library
Local History Division
rpf01558

8 REYNOLDS ARCADE INTERIOR, 1877
Rochester Public Library
Local History Division
rpf00403

10 FOUR CORNERS, 1880
Rochester Public Library
Local History Division
rpf00578

11 MILK DELIVERY SLEIGH
Rochester Public Library
Local History Division
rpf00640

12 STEAM SAWMILL OF C. C. MEYER AND SON
Rochester Public Library
Local History Division
rpf01645

13 MAIN STREET FROM FOUR CORNERS
Rochester Public Library
Local History Division
rpf01137

14 HORSE RACE AT ROCHESTER DRIVING PARK
Rochester Public Library
Local History Division
rpf01111

15 HORSE-DRAWN STREETCAR
Rochester Public Library
Local History Division
rpf00449

16 MAIN AND AQUEDUCT STREETS
Rochester Public Library
Local History Division
rpf01086

17 POLICEMAN ON MAIN AND FITZHUGH
Rochester Public Library
Local History Division
rpf00922

18 FUNERAL OF FREDERICK KISLINGBURY
Rochester Public Library
Local History Division
rpf00548

19 STOREFRONT OF JOSEPH SHATZ MILLINERY
Rochester Public Library
Local History Division
rpf01080

Printed in the USA
CPSIA information can be obtained
at www.ICGtesting.com
JSHW072025140824
68134JS00042B/3793